ENGLISH FOR WORK

BUSINESS
PRESENTATIONS

GW00691238

Anne Freitag-Lawrence

Longman

Pearson Education Limited
Edinburgh Gate, Harlow,
Essex, CM20 2JE, England
and Associated Companies throughout the world

www.longman.com
Copyright © Anne Freitag-Lawrence 2003

First published 2003
Third edition 2005
ISBN   Without audio: 0 582 53960 9
          With audio: 0 582 53962 5

Set in Univers Condensed 10pt
Printed in China.   EPC/03

Designed and typeset by Rock Graphics

Illustrations by Anthony Seldon

Acknowledgements
I would like to thank Ian Badger, Helen Parker and Julie Nowell for their editorial support
through the process of writing this book. In addition, I would especially like to thank
Mary Lazo, Helen Wang and Paul Freitag-Lawrence for their valuable comments and
assistance at different stages of the writing process. I would also like to thank ACE
Education Management Co. Ltd in China for their support while writing this book.

Cover photograph copyright © Getty Images

Contents

Introduction	page 5	

1 Getting Started page 7	**Dialogues 1** Welcoming a speaker Welcoming visitors and introducing the speaker Saying who you are Explaining the reasons for listening Starting with a personal story Starting with an interesting fact	**Dialogues 2** Giving background Explaining the plan for the session Outlining a presentation Questions while you talk Questions at the end Handouts at the end Handouts now
2 Moving on page 15	**Dialogues 1** Using questions to organise Organising points The general to the specific Presenting options Giving your opinion Referring back Changing topic	**Dialogues 2** Reporting bad news Reporting positive information Explaining the meaning of abbreviations Explaining the meaning of specific words/terms Giving examples Repeating your point using different words Expressing possible/likely outcomes Concluding and moving on
3 Numbers page 23	**Dialogues 1** Percentages Fractions Large and small numbers Decimal points Positive and negative numbers Approximate numbers	**Dialogues 2** An increase A decrease Staying the same High and low points Predicting Describing changes
4 Visual Aids page 31	**Dialogues 1** Using slides Changing slides Looking at detail Commenting on the content of a visual Moving between different visual aids Problems	**Dialogues 2** Explaining a graph Using a pie chart Explaining a diagram Describing a flow chart Describing a table
5 Problems and questions page 39	**Dialogues 1** Losing your place in your notes You don't know the English word A deleted or wrong slide Time has run out You have forgotten to say something Making a mistake You are unable to do something you had planned to do	**Dialogues 2** Interruptions to your talk You don't understand a question A question that is not on the topic You don't know the answer to a question An aggressive or difficult question No questions
6 Concluding page 47	**Dialogues 1** Making a final point Giving your professional opinion Summarising main points Summarising advantages and disadvantages Making a recommendation Stating sources and further reading	**Dialogues 2** Telling people how to contact you A final summary Thanking people for listening An informal ending Ending on a positive note Ending with a final thought Ending with a quote

Glossary	page 55	
Answers	page 61	

Introduction

English for Work

The books in this series present and practise spoken English and practical writing for everyday communication; they feature key words and expressions which will help you in a wide range of work situations. The target language is introduced through short dialogues and texts, and developed in language notes and practice exercises.

The dialogues are recorded on an accompanying CD. The accents featured are predominantly British English, but comments on American usage are included in the notes.

At the back of each book there is a glossary which contains highlighted language from the dialogues. Translations of the glossary, in selected languages, can be downloaded from the Longman website, **www.longman-elt.com**.

The series is intended for pre-intermediate/intermediate level learners.

Business Presentations

Business Presentations is suitable for anyone who needs to give presentations in the business world, and for students in adult education classes, schools, colleges and universities.

The book contains a range of language common to all who need to use English to make business presentations. This book gives language and examples for all stages of a business presentation including the introduction, the main body, talking about statistics and even what to do if you have a problem. The book will help you as you prepare and practise your business presentation.

In order to widen your knowledge of the language you might need in your work, you may find it useful to refer to the other titles in the *English for Work* series:

Everyday Business English
Everyday Technical English
Everyday Business Writing

How to use the book

You can work through *Business Presentations* from start to finish or choose a chapter depending on your business need.

Start a chapter by listening to and repeating the *Useful phrases*. Then listen to the dialogues and study the accompanying notes. Certain phrases have been highlighted that have particular language features associated with them. However, it is worthwhile noting other phrases that appear in the dialogues, which are equally important and can also be seen as key phrases. Use a dictionary to check your understanding of the language presented.

On the notes pages you will find boxes containing notes on some differences between everyday British and American usage.

After studying the dialogues and notes, work through the exercises. You can refer back to the dialogues and notes as necessary. Answers and possible responses to the more 'open-ended' exercises are given at the end of the book.

Finally, refer to the glossary at the back of the book and test yourself on your understanding of key expressions. Write translations of these expressions, again using a dictionary if necessary. Visit the *English for Work* page on the Longman website where you will find translations of the key phrases in a number of languages.

You can use this book for self-study or with a teacher. Good luck and enjoy building your 'business presentations' skills!

Anne Freitag-Lawrence, Chengdu, China, 2003

Some recommended materials to accompany the English for Work series:
Longman Business English Dictionary
Penguin Quick Guides: Business English Phrases
Penguin Quick Guides: Business English Verbs
Penguin Quick Guides: Business English Words
Penguin Quick Guides: Computer English

① Getting Started

Some useful phrases.
Listen to the recording and repeat.

It's good to have Paul Kim here from the Korean office.
Welcome, Paul.
Thank you, Sara. It's good to be here today.

Hello. Thank you for coming.
OK. If we're all here, let's begin.
As you all know, I'm Martin Weller, Senior Sales Representative.

I'm talking to you today as the leader of this project.
By the end of this session, you'll know the details of our project.
Sam asked me to explain the project to you.

Right. Today I'd like to talk about the future of our business.
First, I'd like to describe the past.
After that, I'd like to talk about the present.
Finally, I'll try to predict how the business will develop in the future.

If you have any questions, please feel free to stop me.
There'll be time for questions at the end.

Here you are.
Please take one and pass them round.
Did everyone get a copy?

Dialogues 1

Welcoming a speaker

Ⓐ: Well, good morning, everyone. **It's good to have Miguel Ferreira here** from our office in Portugal. Some of you met him last year at the Spring conference. Welcome, Miguel.

Ⓑ: **Thank you, Paul. It's great to be back** in the UK.

Welcoming visitors and introducing the speaker

Hello. Thank you all for coming. I hope you had a good journey here. There are some drinks on the table. **Please help yourselves.**

Right. If everyone's ready, let's start. I'd like to introduce our speaker today, Mrs Samantha Singh, Marketing Director of our company. She'll be talking to us about marketing in a global context.

Saying who you are

Good afternoon. It's great to be here today. **As you all know, I'm the Head of the Design Department.** I've been in this job for four years. Before that I worked for another very successful company in France for five years. **I'm talking to you today as the manager of the team** which developed this new product.

Explaining the reasons for listening

By the end of this session, you'll know enough about the new product to be able to sell it with confidence to our customers. You'll know where the idea came from, how it was designed and how it can benefit our customers.

Starting with a personal story

How do we avoid problems? When I got out of my car this morning, I forgot to switch off the lights. However, an alarm in my car warned me that I had left them on. That means that when I leave here today my car will actually start.

So, the alarm reminded me about my mistake and I was able to act before it became an issue. That's what we need in our company – systems that will warn us and show us potential problems, which we can then prevent. That's what I am going to talk about today.

Starting with an interesting fact

I read something interesting the other day. Did you know that the tunnel which links England and France, was constructed using 13 000 engineers, technicians and workers? This showed amazing organisation and proves that cooperation between companies in different countries can achieve excellent results. So, let's think about this example as we discuss our joint venture project with our partner company.

Notes

It's good to have Miguel Ferreira here ...

Other phrases for introducing a speaker:
I'd like to introduce Mrs Samantha Singh,
Marketing Director of our company.
I'd like to welcome Sam Brandt.
It's a pleasure to welcome Greg Riconda.

Thank you, Paul. It's great to be back ...

Other ways of thanking someone:
Thank you. I'm glad to be here.
Thanks. It's a pleasure to be here.
Thank you for giving me this opportunity to
speak to you today.

Hello. Thank you all for coming.

Some other phrases for greeting people:
Good morning, everyone. Welcome.
Hello. It's good to see you all here.
For a bigger, more formal presentation,
greetings could include the following:
Good evening, ladies and gentlemen.

Please help yourselves.

Other ways of inviting people to take things
include:
Please take a leaflet.
Help yourselves to a brochure.

Right. If everyone's ready, let's start.

Other ways of getting people's attention so
that you can start:
Fine. If we're all here, I'll begin.
OK. Let's get started/Let's make a start.

As you all know, ...

You may use this phrase to make your
listeners feel included. Other similar phrases
include:
As I think you know, ...
As you may know, ...
As I'm sure you know, ...

... I'm the Head of the Design Department.

The simplest way of introducing yourself to
people is to use *I'm ...*
I'm Sam Wang – name
I'm the Assistant Marketing Manager – job title
I'm Paul Schmidt, Senior Sales Executive –
name and title.

I'm talking to you today as the manager of the team ...

Sometimes you won't need to introduce
yourself, because you know people already.
You might, however, like to say why you are
talking or why you were chosen to give the
presentation.

By the end of this session, ...

A presentation can be called a *session* (as in
this dialogue) or a *talk*.

... you'll know enough about the product to be able to sell it ...

Will can be used to make a promise or a
prediction. Here, the speaker is promising or
predicting what the listeners will learn from
the talk. Another example is:
By the end of this session, you'll know how to
follow our new sales procedure.

How do we avoid problems?

Using a personal story or interesting fact is a
good way to get the interest of the audience
at the beginning of a talk. A direct question is
an effective way to introduce a personal
story or interesting fact.
Did you know that the tunnel which links
England and France was constructed using
13 000 engineers, technicians and workers?

I read something interesting the other day.

This phrase is another way of introducing a
story or interesting fact. Other expressions:
A funny thing happened to me the other day ...
On the way here, I saw ...
I noticed in the news last week ...

British/American differences

British	American
Hello. Thank you all for coming.	*Hi. Thanks for coming.*

Note: American business presentations can be
more informal than British ones. Very formal
presentations would generally be very similar
in Britain and America beginning, *'Welcome,*
ladies and gentlemen'.

British	American
I forgot to switch off the lights.	*I forgot to turn off the lights.* (also used in British English)
organisation	*organization*

9

Dialogues 2

Giving background

Sam asked me to present my ideas for a new telephone system. As you know there have been problems with the old system – we've lost calls, we've had no record of those lost calls and overall the system can't manage the large number of callers. I've spent the last two months researching the different systems available. **Today I'd like to present a solution** to you.

Explaining the plan for the session

Right. Today I'd like to present the new policy and especially the changes that have been made over the last two months. **I hope that you'll give your ideas and comments.** **If there is anything else you'd like to bring up**, we can talk about it at the end. If there isn't time at the end, you can always email me.

Outlining a presentation

There are some important issues I want to go through this morning. **First, I'd like to outline the main areas of growth.** After that I'd like to explain how this growth will affect the company's five-year plan. Finally, I want to focus on the next financial year.

Questions while you talk

OK. You all have a copy of the handout with the graphs and statistics. I'll go through the main points on the handout and explain the graphs and statistics. These will help us to understand the situation as it is now. **If you have any questions, please feel free to stop me.**

Questions at the end

After my general introduction, I'd like to outline the new sales plan. This will take about thirty to forty minutes. After you have heard about the new plan, I'm sure you'll have questions. **I'll leave fifteen or twenty minutes at the end for questions**, so if anything is unclear please ask me then.

Handouts now

Here are some tables which illustrate what I'm saying. I have copies of these and the statistics I've mentioned on this handout. Here you are. **Please take one** each and pass them round. Did everyone get a copy?

Handouts at the end

I will be covering a lot of topics in this presentation and will be giving you some figures and statistics. However, don't worry about taking notes while I talk. **I have a handout with the main points of my presentation**, which I'll give you at the end. **The handout contains all the statistics as well**.

Notes

Sam asked me to present my ideas …

Other ways of explaining why you are talking:

I promised to report the results of our survey to you.

I've been asked to speak to you about …

Smart Inc has invited me here to present …

Today I'd like to present a solution …

This is a phrase for explaining what you're going to do in the talk. Other phrases from the dialogues that state intention are:

Today I'd like to talk about …

I want to focus on …

Right.

There are several words you can use to fill a gap or to start:

OK/All right/Well/So/Fine

But remember not to use these words too much!

I hope that you'll give your ideas and comments.

Other ways of inviting people to comment as you speak:

Please make comments as I talk.

Please feel free to give me your feedback.

If there is anything else you'd like to bring up, …

If phrases can be used to make polite suggestions:

If you have any other comments, …

If you have any other important points to raise, …

First, I'd like to outline the main areas of growth.

To outline means to summarise. When you outline the points you will cover in your talk you can use the following phrases:

First – Firstly/To begin with/To start with …

After that – Next/I'd also like to …

Finally – Lastly/The last point/Last of all …

If you have any questions, please feel free to stop me.

Other phrases which invite people to ask questions in the middle of your talk:

I'm happy to answer any questions as I talk.

Please feel free to ask questions as we go along.

I'll leave fifteen or twenty minutes at the end for questions, …

Other similar phrases include:

I'd be happy to answer any questions at the end.

There'll be time at the end for questions and comments.

There will be time for questions at the end.

Please save any questions for the end of the talk.

Please take one …

You can also use a question form:

Would you like one of these?

Would you like to take one as I pass them around?

I have a handout with the main points of my presentation, …

Other ways of telling people that you have information to give them:

I have copies of the statistics and tables. I'll give these to you later.

The figures are on a sheet which you can have later.

The handout contains all the statistics as well.

As well means also. For example:

The handout also contains all the statistics.

British/American differences

British	American
I've spent the last two months	*I spent the last two months* (American English usually uses the simple past tense.)
programme, p12	*program*

(Note: British English uses programme when referring to a programme of events or a television programme but program for anything relating to computers.)

Practice

1 Match a sentence or phrase on the left with one from the right.

1	Please help yourselves	a	describe the new proposal.
2	If we're all here,	b	Thank you Michel. It's good to be here.
3	I'd like to start by	c	to the brochures at the back.
4	I have a handout with the statistics on.	d	let's make a start.
5	I'd like to welcome Sonja Malden.	e	Please take one as I pass them around.
6	After that I'd like to	f	please feel free to ask me.
7	Today, I'd like to talk about	g	outlining the plan for the day.
8	If you have any questions,	h	the success we've had with after-sales.

2 Choose a verb from the box to complete each of the sentences below.

introduce	~~begin~~	take	have
present		leave	like

EXAMPLE: If we're all here, I'll . . . . . . begin . . . .

a   It's good to . . . . Shireen here from the Head Office.

b   I have the figures for the last three months to . . . . to you.

c   Would you like to . . . . a handout?

d   I'd . . . . to talk today about last year's sales figures.

e   I plan to . . . . about twenty minutes for questions at the end.

f   I'd like to . . . . our speaker today.

3 Fill the gaps in the sentences below with a preposition.

on	from	by	as	at	on	by	~~for~~

EXAMPLE: Thank you . . . for . . . . . coming.

a   There are copies . . . . the table.

b   I'd like to start . . . . outlining the changes.

c   It's good to have Michelle here . . . . the Malaysian office.

d   We can discuss any questions . . . . the end.

e   I want to focus . . . . the five-year plan.

f   . . . . the end of this session, you'll be able to teach your staff how to use this programme.

g   I'm talking to you today . . . . the designer of this new marketing plan.

4 The following sentences are mixed up. Put the words into the correct order.

EXAMPLE: for / to / thank / like / all / you/ coming

I'd *like to thank you all for coming.* . . . .

1 points / handout / of / have / with / my / the / a / main / presentation

I . . . .

2 customer / care / here / explain / to

I'm . . . .

3 Malaysian / I'm / office / the / Mohammed / from

Good morning. . . . .

4 the / read / interesting / day / something / other

I . . . .

5 outline / begin / I'd / proposal / to / with / like / the

To . . . . , ...

6 leader / you / sure / I'm / I'm / know / project / the

As . . . . , ...

5 Complete the sentences with the correct word.

EXAMPLE: It's good to . . . . . *meet* . . . . you. have / take / meet

a Did everyone . . . . a handout ? give / get / go

b Don't . . . . about taking notes. worry / forget / think

c Please . . . . yourselves. meet / have / help

d Please feel . . . . to stop me. expensive / free / open

e I'd like to . . . . the past. let / happen / describe

f I want to . . . . on the results first. look / worry / focus

6 **Write down a possible phrase or sentence from the dialogues for each of the following. Use the words provided in brackets.**

EXAMPLE: You are a sales manager from the Frankfurt office. Not everyone knows you. How do you introduce yourself at the beginning of a presentation? (I'm …)

Hello. I'm Dieter Kuhl from the Frankfurt office.

1 David Wang has welcomed you and thanked you for coming to talk today. How do you reply? (glad)

....

2 You want to get everyone's attention so that you can start your meeting. What can you say? (here/begin)

....

3 You have handouts that you want to give people. What can you say? (take)

....

4 In your presentation, you plan to explain the problems of the old process and then present the new process. How can you explain what you are going to do? (First/After that)

....

5 How can you tell your listeners that there will be time for questions at the end? (plan/leave)

....

7 **Complete the following introduction with appropriate words from the unit.**

S: Well, If everyone's ① .... ② .... start. It's great to have Liu Wei here ③ ....the office in Beijing. As you ④ ...., he is the Director of Marketing and has achieved excellent results.

LW: Good afternoon. Thank you Sam. I'm ⑤ .... to be here today. OK, today I'd ⑥ .... to talk about the developments in the Beijing office. We've had to develop quickly to meet the demands of the market and it's been hard work but very rewarding. In my presentation this afternoon I'd like to ⑦ .... three main points. ⑧ ...., I'll briefly outline our small beginnings two years ago; ⑨ .... I'll explain how we adapted the RB409 range to suit the local market and ⑩............... I'll show our success. If you have any questions, there'll be ⑪............... at the end.

Before I start, I ⑫ .... a handout for you. It has the graphs and main notes on it. Would you like to ⑬ .... one? Here you are.

② Moving on

Some useful phrases.
Listen to the recording and repeat.

So, what is the solution to this problem?
Well, there are two possible solutions.
The first solution is to train more staff.
The second solution is to buy a better system.

So, that's an overall look at our financial situation.
Let's now look at predictions for next year.
Unfortunately, we've just lost our oldest customer.
The good news is that we've just signed two new customers.

To sum up, we've done better this year than ever before.
I'd now like to move on to the future of our company.
I said earlier that Hooper's used to be the leaders – not any more.

LIFO stands for Last In First Out.
Follow-up – that's calling a customer after they've bought a product from us.
We must improve this system quickly otherwise we'll lose more customers.
In other words, if we don't improve, we may have to cancel the promotion.

Dialogues 1

Using questions

It's important to know what customers think of our new product, so we've done some market research. Now we need to assess this research. In order to do that, **we must ask ourselves these questions.** What does the customer really want? Does the product really meet those needs? How can we improve? **Let me answer each of these questions one by one.** First, what does the customer really want? Well, our research shows that ...

Organising points

The first problem is call-response times – that is the time it takes to answer the phones. Many customers complained of waiting for a long time for the phone to be answered. For example, several customers reported waiting for up to forty minutes. As a result of this, we've probably lost many customers to other companies. **Another problem is following up on calls.**

From the general to the specific

So, **that's an overall look at the marketing campaign and now for the details.** We need to look at each part of the marketing plan in turn and make decisions about each so that we can progress.

Presenting options

As far as I see, **there are three options.** First, we can continue as we are for another year and then discuss the options again later. Second, we can update the system we have, which will last for another two to three years. Third, we could buy a completely new system which should last for at least seven to ten years.

Giving your opinion

We need to think about how much money we have at the moment. **In my opinion, we are in a strong financial position** and so I think we should invest in a new building. **If we build now, we will be ready for the expansion** we are planning over the next few years.

Referring back

There are some things that we need to do better this year. For example, **I said earlier that security wasn't very good last year.** This year we need to improve it. We need to examine what wasn't good and work out ways to improve.

Changing topic

OK. I've explained how we organised the project last year. **I'd now like to change direction** and talk about our plans for this year's project. We have some good ideas and I feel very positive about the start we've already made.

Notes

… we must ask ourselves these questions.

Questions can be introduced in other ways.
For example:
There are three questions I'd like to ask/answer.
There are several questions we need to think about.

Let me answer each of these questions one by one.

This is a way of emphasising the order of the talk by telling the listeners that you will answer each question in order. You could also say:
I'll answer these questions in turn.

The first problem is call-response times …

The points in your talk can be organised using words and phrases such as:
The first reason is/First …
Another problem/The next reason is/In addition, …
As a result/Following on from that …
Finally/My last reason …

Another problem is following up on calls.

To *follow up* is to maintain contact with a person in order to give them further advice and to make sure that earlier actions have been successful.

… that's an overall look at the marketing campaign and now for the details.

Some other similar phrases:
That's a general look at our plan, now let's look at the details.
That's the issue in general, now let's look at the first problem in detail.
Having given an overview, let's now turn to specific questions/problems/issues.

… there are three options.

Options are *choices.*
Some other ways to present options:
There are four alternatives.
There seem to be two choices.
We can update the system.
We could buy a completely new system.

In my opinion, we are in a strong financial position …

Other ways of giving your personal opinion:
I think …
It seems to me that …
The obvious/best choice would be …
Personally, I would recommend …
As far as I see it …

If we build now, we will be ready for the expansion …

Using a conditional sentence (*If* + present tense + future) is a good way to introduce choice, options, advice and opinions.
If we buy the new system later, we won't be ready …

… I said earlier that security wasn't very good last year.

To refer back to earlier points you could also say:
In my last point, I mentioned that …
As I've already explained …
At the beginning of the talk I said …

I'd now like to change direction …

This phrase makes it clear that you are changing to a new topic. Other possible phrases:
I now want to move to the next point …
Let's move on to the next question/issue.
Let's turn to the third advantage of this plan.

British/American differences	
British	**American**
organising	*organizing*
at the moment	*right now*
emphasising	*emphasizing*

Dialogues 2

Reporting bad news

Unfortunately, the number of new customers who joined our scheme last year **was below target.** This is disappointing because we spent a lot of money on marketing and staff training, and everyone expected better results.

Reporting good news

However, **the good news is that** so far this year **we've nearly doubled sales** of the new office furniture range. So, we've started the year well and must make sure we continue this progress throughout the year.

Explaining the meaning of abbreviations

So, what's our plan for the future of this company? Well, first – over the next two years, we want to introduce some new OTC drugs – **OTC stands for over-the-counter drugs.** In other words, drugs which customers can buy without needing to get a prescription first.

Explaining the meaning of specific words and terms

We need to think about how we can improve our service to customers. As I mentioned earlier, the biggest area for improvement is call-response times – **that's the time it takes someone to answer the phone in our call centre.**

Giving examples

Apparently, many customers use our accounting programme for their home accounts. **For example,** they use our package to organise their regular payments such as bills and they also monitor their savings. They also think that our programme is easy to use. For instance, they like the clear instruction boxes which appear on screen.

Repeating your point using different words

Complaints from customers are increasing. Most complaints focus on waiting times and lack of information. **In short, we need to improve our customer service.** Receiving complaints from customers is not good for business. We need to improve our waiting times and provide clearer and more regular information.

Expressing possible outcomes

These are our predictions. **We will produce the new software** by the end of the year. However, we know how markets change and so **we may find ourselves marketing it in a different way.**

Concluding a section and moving on

To sum up, last month's sales doubled and **this is excellent** **for this time of year.** This increase was probably due to the very cold weather we had.
Next, I'd like to move on and look at the sales for the following six months. As you know, we're doing well as a company but we need to continue this increase in sales and that means everyone must work even harder.

Notes

Unfortunately the number of new customers ... was below target.

Other useful expressions:
I'm sorry to say that ...
Sadly, we will not be able to ...
It is unfortunate that ...

... the good news is that we've nearly doubled sales ...

Other phrases to introduce good news:
I'm pleased to say that ...
You'll be happy to know that ...

OTC stands for over-the-counter drugs.

We use *stands for* to explain abbreviations.
WTO stands for World Trade Organisation.
IMF stands for International Monetary Fund.

... that's the time it takes someone to answer the phone in our call centre.

The phrase *That is/That's* can be used to introduce an explanation.

For example, ...

Expressions used to introduce an example:
Such as ...
For instance ...

In short, we need to improve our customer service.

You may want to repeat a point in different words in order to make sure everyone has understood or to emphasise the point. You could also use:
Again, ...
In other words, ...
That is to say, ...
To put it another way, ...

We will produce the new software ...

Will/will not (won't) can be used for predictions.
There will be an increase in sales.
There won't be any opportunities for further development.

... we may find ourselves marketing it in a different way.

May is used to indicate outcomes that are possible but not certain. Possibility can also be expressed using *might* or *could*:
There could be positive results from this.
There may/might not be positive results from this.

To sum up, last month's sales doubled ...

When you've finished presenting a point, you'll probably want to summarise the key points for the listener. You can also do this with phrases such as:
In short, ...
Therefore, ...

... this is excellent ...

Ways to express your opinion on the information you have presented:
This is excellent/very good/better than we had expected.
This is disappointing/This is worse than expected/This is not very good.

... for this time of year.

Other ways to indicate time:
For the next six months ...
For this period ...
For this point in the five-year business plan ...
Over this two-year period ...

Next I'd like to move on and look at the sales ...

This phrase can be used to show that you are changing topic. Other useful phrases:
Let's move on now to ...
Shall we now turn to ...
Now we'll move on to ...

British/American differences

British	American
call centre	*call center*
... for their home accounts	*... for their home financial recordkeeping/ bookkeeping ...*
Sadly, we will not be able to ... (*Sadly* is not used in American English in this way)	*Unfortunately/regrettably, we won't be able to ...* (also used in British English)
summarise	*summarize*

Practice

1 Choose the best word or phrase to complete each sentence.

EXAMPLE: The first . p̲r̲o̲b̲l̲e̲m̲ . . . . is the lack of staff.

      a problem   b solution   c overall   d direction

1   I'd now like to change . . . . and talk about solutions.

    a aim   b turns   c direction   d options

2   That's an overall look, now let's focus on the . . . .

    a technical   b necessary   c continue   d details

3   EU . . . . European Union.

    a looks for   b stands for   c is for   d represents for

4   There are only two . . . . First, we can upgrade our current system or second, we can buy a new one.

    a behaviours   b possible   c instances   d options

5   To . . . . up, I have explained the problems and given three solutions.

    a build   b sum   c finalise   d end

6   OK. We've looked at customers' complaints. I'd now like to . . . . to looking at our retraining programme.

    a change   b sign   c turn   d move

7   It . . . . to me that there are many opportunities for us to grow.

    a seems   b could   c might   d should

2 Match a sentence or phrase from the left with one from the right.

1	MD stands for	a	For example, it will help us to look at customer information much quicker.
2	I've explained how we worked last year.	b	in turn.
3	The new information system will help us a lot.	c	we have a lot of people interested in this idea.
4	I'd like to move on now	d	these important questions.
5	As I said earlier in the talk	e	I now want to turn to our plans for this year.
6	I'll answer each question	f	the majority of customers were not satisfied with our service.
7	We must ask ourselves	g	Managing Director.
8	I'm sorry to say that	h	and look at another answer to this problem.

3 Put the following words and phrases into the correct gaps in the paragraph.

As a result	The next	First	In other words
Next	Third	For example	

The next . . . . . . problem is follow-up. (i) . . . ., phoning the customer again to make sure that they're happy with our service. Why is follow up important? (ii) . . . ., it makes the customer feel that we care (iii) . . . . it makes them loyal to us. (iv) . . . . we can solve problems before they become too big. (v) . . . ., last week we phoned Mr Smith and found that his order had not been delivered. He'd tried to call us but no one had answered, so he was very pleased that we had called him. (vi) . . . . of this, he's now very happy and will probably tell his friends about us.

4 Complete the questions using a word from the box. Some words may be used more than once.

Why	How	What	Does	Where

EXAMPLE: _What_ . . . . options do we have?

a . . . . does the customer want from our product?

b . . . . can we solve this problem?

c . . . . the new telephone system meet our needs?

d . . . . is there such an increase in returned goods?

e . . . . many customers have we lost?

f . . . . do teenagers prefer to shop?

g . . . . do so many women prefer this product?

5 Put each of the verbs into the past.

EXAMPLE: Two years ago we (introduce) _introduced_ . . . a new computer system.

1 Last month our response times (be) . . . . better.

2 At the beginning of the talk, I (explain) . . . . our new vision.

3 I said at the beginning that we (have) . . . . three new products.

4 Last year we (sell) . . . . more than the previous year.

5 Earlier in my talk, I (mention) . . . . that there were four points.

6 Put the following questions into the correct order.

EXAMPLE: do / customers / so / why / many / complain

Why do so many customers complain ....?

1   do / new / our / product / what / you / know / about

. . . . ?

2   increase / can / sales / how / we

. . . . ?

3   product / is / to / buy / our / who / going /

. . . . ?

4   product / what / the / is / new

. . . . ?

5   we / complete / when / changes / the / can

. . . . ?

6   start / we / where / shall

. . . . ?

7 Start each sentence with an appropriate word from the box.

Again	For instance	In short	I think	As a result of this

a   . . . . , we should employ more staff.   (your opinion)

b   . . . . , there are two choices.   (summary)

c   . . . . , we now have to start again.   (consequence)

d   . . . . , this is our only chance.   (repeating in different words)

e   . . . . , they think our programme is
                                                easy to use.   (example)

③ Numbers

Only 27 per cent of customers responded.
Only about one quarter of our customers replied.
About 40 per cent of people rent their homes.
Over two-fifths of the population rent their accommodation.

The most expensive car in our range costs $350 000.
We only sold 230 last year.
An estimated 1.2 million people answered our questionnaire.
The average home in Europe has 2.4 children.

Around 350 people applied for the new jobs.
Just over half of them were graduates.
Just less than two-thirds of them were women.

The graph shows a rise in the number of customers.
There was a fall in the number of complaints last year.
The number of new customers has stayed the same.

You can see that the sale of coffee peaked last month.
The graph shows that the sale of tea reached a low point last month.
There was a dramatic rise in the number of people visiting our website last year.

Dialogues 1

Percentages

From this table you can see the shopping habits of men and women. First is planned or unplanned shopping. You can see that **69 per cent of male shoppers** only buy what they've planned to buy, whereas 76 per cent of female shoppers buy things **on impulse**. Second is response to special offers: 62 per cent of women react positively to special offers and so do 51 per cent of men.

Fractions

We asked 100 people what they thought of the new pens. **Two-thirds of those questioned said that they liked the new colours**, and three-quarters of them said they liked the new shape. However, one-quarter said that they didn't look modern and about one-half said that they looked cheap.

Large and small numbers

Last year we had 332 students in each of our three schools. This year with six schools we have a total of 960 students. Next year, **we hope to have 1 530 in nine schools**. As student numbers increase so does our turnover. Last year our turnover was $4 000 000 and we expect that next year it will be about $6 000 000.

Decimal points

We all know that according to the law we must check the temperature of our storage fridges every day. For the model of fridge that we use, **the temperature must be between 4.3° and 5.6° centigrade**. If the temperature of the fridges falls above or below this temperature, you must inform a manager.

Positive and negative numbers

Take a look at the financial figures. I predict that **we'll make a loss of €50 000 this year**. **You can see the number -50 000 in the third column**. However, **next year we expect to break even**. The following year **we expect to make a profit** of €70 000.

Approximate numbers

Around 300 people responded to our questionnaire. Just over half of them were under the age of eighteen. **About 30 per cent were between eighteen and forty** and less than 20 per cent were over forty.

Notes

... 69 per cent of male shoppers ...

The preposition *of* is used with percentages:
76 per cent of female shoppers ...
84 per cent of employees ...
43 per cent is usually written as *43%*.

... on impulse.

To buy something *on impulse* is to make a spontaneous, unplanned purchase.

Two-thirds of those questioned said that they liked the new colours, ...

Say fractions as follows:
½ *half/a half/one-half*
⅓ *a third/one-third*   ⅔ *two-thirds*
¼ *quarter/a quarter/*   ¾ *three-quarters*
   one-quarter   ⅜ *three-eighths*
⅛ *an eighth/one-eighth*

As with percentages, the preposition *of* is used when describing fractions. For example:
Three quarters of people ...
Four fifths of our customers ...

... we hope to have 1 530 in nine schools.

Say numbers as follows:
2.50	*two point five oh*
25	*twenty-five*
250	*two hundred and fifty*
2 500	*two thousand five hundred* (you can also say *twenty-five hundred*)
25 000	*twenty-five thousand*
250 000	*two hundred and fifty thousand*
2 500 000	*two million five hundred thousand* or *two and a half million*

... the temperature must be between 4.3° and 5.6° centigrade.

Say numbers with a decimal point as follows:
54.749 fifty-four point seven four nine
54.750 fifty-four point seven five oh
With amounts of money, the numbers after the point are read as follows:
$45.50 forty-five dollars fifty cents
€57.25 fifty-seven euros twenty-five cents
Temperatures are read as follows:
4.3°C four point three degrees centigrade

... we'll make a loss of 50 000 this year.
... next year we expect to break even.
... we expect to make a profit ...

When you *make a loss*, your income is less than your expenditure.
When you *break even*, your income is the same as your expenditure.
When you *make a profit*, your income is more than your expenditure.

You can see the number -50 000 in the third column.

Negative numbers are read as follows:
-50 000 *minus fifty thousand*
-7.4   *minus seven point four*

Around 300 people responded to our questionnaire.

Around is used to talk about approximate numbers. Other useful expressions:
About/approximately/roughly
Just over/a little more than/more than
Less than/just under/under

About 30 per cent were between eighteen and forty ...

It is important when speaking to make a clear difference between numbers ending with *–teen* and those ending with *–ty*. You can make the difference clear with stress as follows (the part of the number in bold is the part to stress):
13	*thir**teen***	30	***thir**ty*
14	*four**teen***	40	***for**ty*
15	*fif**teen***	50	***fif**ty*

British/American differences

British	American
colours	*colors*
332 = three hundred and thirty-two	*three hundred thirty-two*
250 000 = two hundred and fifty thousand	*two hundred fifty thousand*
fridge (not used in American English.)	*refrigerator* (also used in British English.)
centigrade	Note: American English generally uses the Fahrenheit scale, but some international businesses may use centigrade.

◉Dialogues 2

An increase

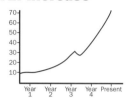

This chart shows a significant rise in the number of companies selling cheap modern furniture. Two years ago there were thirty major companies selling this type of furniture. **This year the number has gone up to seventy.** That means that the competition in the market has more than doubled in twelve months.

A decrease

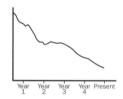

There has been a significant decrease in the number of people with more than one child over the last five years. As a result, **the number of children going to Primary school will also fall.** This will affect our sales of Primary school books and in the future it will also affect our sales of Secondary school books.

Staying the same

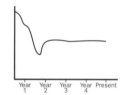

It's interesting to note that **the number of staff has stayed the same** for the past three years. Basically the demand for trained instructors has stabilised and the market has levelled out.

High and low points

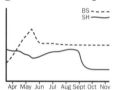

Sales of Brighter Smile toothpaste peaked in May of last year. However, Shine Hair shampoo is not doing so well. It entered a trough in October last year. Sales are still below expectation.

Predicting

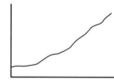

We can see that the number of people who own a private car has increased significantly in Kenya over the last few years. **I believe there'll be a dramatic rise in private car owners** **over the next few years.**

Describing changes

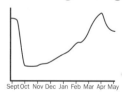

Last year was a very unusual year for us. In October, **sales fell dramatically.** Look at this trough in the graph. After November, **sales began to increase gradually.** Then there was a dramatic increase as you can see with this peak in April. After April, **sales** fell again and then **stayed more or less the same** for the rest of the year.

Notes

The chart shows a significant rise ...

Here are some other ways to describe an increase (adjective + noun):
A dramatic increase.
A sharp rise.
A small increase.

This year the number has gone up to seventy.

Some more ways to describe an increase (subject + verb + adverb):
The number went up sharply.
Sales rose dramatically/increased significantly.
The number has doubled/tripled.

There has been a significant decrease in the number of people with more than one child ...

Here are some other ways to describe a decrease (adjective + noun):
A dramatic decrease.
A sharp fall.
A slight fall.

... the number of children going to Primary school will also fall.

Some more ways to describe a decrease (verb + adverb):
Sales fell sharply/went down significantly/ reduced dramatically.

... the number of staff has stayed the same ...

Here are some ways of describing something which stays the same:
The number has reached a plateau.
The number has levelled out.
Staff numbers have stabilised.

Sales of Brighter Smile toothpaste peaked in May ...

Peaked is used here to describe the highest point in the number of sales, after peaking numbers always go down. Here are some other examples:
Sales peaked.
Sales reached a high point.
And some ways to describe low points in a graph:
Sales reached a trough.
Sales reached a low point.

I believe there'll be a dramatic rise in private car owners ...

Other ways of giving your opinion about the future:
I expect there to be ...
I predict there'll be ...
This leads one to expect that there'll be ...

... over the next few years.

Other expressions you can use are as follows:
Over the following months ...
For the next three years ...
In the coming months/years ...

... sales fell dramatically.

To describe a decrease, you can also say:
There was a drop in sales.
Sales dropped.

... sales began to increase gradually.

Here are some other ways of explaining a gradual increase or decrease (adjective + noun):
A gradual increase
A steady fall
And other ways (verb + adverb):
The graph rose steadily/fell gradually.

... sales stayed more or less the same.

More or less could be replaced here using:
roughly or *approximately*

British/American differences	
British	**American**
This chart shows a significant rise ...	This chart shows a significant increase ... (also used in British English)
The number of children going to Primary school will fall.	The number of children going to elementary school will go down. (go down is also used in British English)
The past three years.	The last three years. (also used in British English – this would be more usual in American English)
Sales stayed the same.	also: Sales remained flat.
stabilised	stabilized
levelled	leveled

Practice

1 Write down how you would say the following numbers:

EXAMPLE: 36.45   *thirty six point four five ...*

1   ¼ of all shoppers   . . . .

2   $45.70   . . . .

3   ⅞ of all men   . . . .

4   35% of children   . . . .

5   -65.02   . . . .

6   423 000   . . . .

7   ⅔ of the population   . . . .

8   243   . . . .

2 Complete each sentence below with a word from the box. Use each word once

than	more than	just under	roughly	less than	over	around

EXAMPLE: (345–355)   ..*roughly*........ 350 people applied for the new post.

a   (63 out of 100)   . . . . half of the applicants were well qualified.

b   Sadly, less . . . . a quarter of the employees attended the presentation.

c   (33%)   A little . . . . 30 per cent of them were in the forty-five to fifty-five age group.

d   (48%)   . . . . 50 per cent of them were under thirty years old.

e   We received . . . . 1500 – 1600 questionnaires back from customers.

f   (71%)   . . . . three-quarters of men said they prefer diet drinks.

3 Use words from the box below to describe each graph.

stay the same ~~rise~~ decline	dramatically
drop peak	steadily
	~~gradually~~

EXAMPLE:

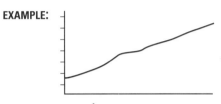

.Sales. rose. gradually..

1

. . . .

3

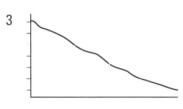

. . . .

2

. . . .

4

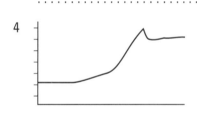

. . . .

4 Change the noun form into the verb form.

EXAMPLE: There was a **dramatic increase** in the number of sales.

The number of sales increased dramatically. . . . .

a   The graph shows a sharp fall in the sales of Stay Fresh washing powder.

. . . .

b   We can see a significant rise in ticket sales.

. . . .

c   There was a gradual decrease in the number of dog owners.

. . . .

d   There were twice as many complaints.

   . . . .

e   There was a steady drop in petrol consumption.

   . . . .

f   There was a dramatic increase in the number of private cars.

   . . . .

g   The number of sales reached a level. (to level out)

   . . . .

5 Fill the gaps in the texts below with a word from the box.

a

out	to be	increase	in	peak	rise	~~show~~	to

The graph . .shows. . . . . . our book sales last year. From January ⁱ. . . . .
March sales ⁱⁱ. . . . . gradually from 20 000 to 35 000. After March, sales
continued ⁱⁱⁱ. . . . . steadily to 50 000 ⁱᵛ. . . . . June. From June to
August, sales levelled ᵛ. . . . . The lowest point in the year ᵛⁱ. . . . .
October. Our best month was December when sales ᵛⁱⁱ. . . . . at 70 000.

b

profit	make	break	prediction	expect

Let's take a look at the financial figures. Unfortunately, figures were below
ⁱ. . . . . last year. In fact, we ⁱⁱ. . . . . a loss of $20 000. However, this
year, predictions are that we will ⁱⁱⁱ. . . . . even. If things go as we
ⁱᵛ. . . . . we will be making a ᵛ. . . . . in two years time.

c

following	in	less	perdict	as	next

Having looked at the data, I ⁱ. . . . . there will be a steady increase in sales
over the ⁱⁱ. . . . . six months. The drop ⁱⁱⁱ. . . . . sales over the last
three months is unusual and will not continue. Sales are more or ⁱᵛ. . . . .
stable now and as far ᵛ. . . . . I can see, they will start to rise gradually over
the ᵛⁱ. . . . . months.

4 Visual Aids

Some useful phrases.
Listen to the recording and repeat.

From this slide you can see that there are three options.
On the next slide, you can see this year's sales figures.
Let's look at these figures more closely.
It's interesting to note that sales have increased dramatically.

I'll do a quick breakdown for you on the flipchart.
Let me find the relevant slide.
Let me show you that clip again.

This graph shows the cash flow for the last quarter.
75 per cent of readers like the gardening feature.
The main building is at the bottom of the plan.
Extras are listed on the left of the table.

First, the customer places an order.
The salesperson then sends the order to dispatch.
When the order is ready it is delivered to the customer.

FROM THIS SLIDE YOU CAN SEE CLEARLY HOW THE NEW PROCESS WORKS.

Dialogues 1

Introducing a slide

This morning I'm going to talk about the computer software market. **You can see from this slide that I'm going to cover three points.** I'll leave this up as I talk so that you can follow the points.

Changing slides

OK. **On the next slide you can see** a picture of the new model which will be launched next week. Doesn't it look good? And here, on this slide is a diagram of the inside and how it actually works. You can see that the mechanism inside is quite complex.

Now, let's look at the programme for the launch which is on the following slide.

Looking at detail

Let's look at the figures on this slide more closely. In the first quarter of last year, sales of our lead home improvement magazine doubled due to the booming economy and our successful advertising campaign. You can see that in the same quarter, sales of our women's fashion magazine dropped slightly due to new competition.

Commenting on the content of a visual

Looking at this graph **it's interesting to note that the increase in sales happened** just **after our** special advertising **campaign**. The worrying thing is that there was also an increase in our competitors' sales at the same time. It's surprising to see how quickly our competitors reacted to the campaign.

Moving between different visual aids

Ⓐ: Are there any questions?
Ⓑ: Your graph is very helpful but **can you just clarify how you worked out the figures?**
Ⓐ: Certainly. **I'll do a quick break down for you on the flipchart.**
Ⓒ: Could you explain again how the market is divided up?
Ⓐ: Yes, **let me find the relevant slide.**

Problems

Ⓐ: Right. I'll just put this up on the screen so that you can see it. [Nothing appears on screen] Oh dear. Unfortunately, **the projector doesn't seem to be working. Does anyone know how it works?**
Ⓑ: Are you sure the power is on?
[speaker adjusts plugs and switches]
Ⓐ: Ah .... Now it's working.
Ⓒ: Excuse me. I can't see it very clearly.
Ⓐ: I'm sorry. **I'll adjust it. Is that better?**
Ⓒ: Yes, thanks. That's fine.

Notes

You can see from this slide that I'm going to cover three points.

Other ways of asking listeners to look at your visuals:

Take a look at this graph and you'll see …

This slide shows the …

As you can see from the slide/graph/chart …

On the next slide you can see …

Here are some more expressions you can use as you change slides:

Here is the next slide. This shows …

Let's look at another example of this which is on the following slide.

Let's look at the figures on this slide more closely.

Here is another way of asking people to look at detail:

I'd also like to draw your attention to …

Right here you can see …

Notice the …

… it's interesting to note that the increase in sales happened after our campaign.

These expressions can be used to give your opinion about the content of a graph, table etc.

It's interesting/worrying/surprising/of concern + to note/see/realise …

The worrying/interesting/surprising thing is that …

… can you just clarify how you worked out the figures?

Other ways of asking for clarification:

Can you tell us more about that?

Can you explain that again?

Can you go over that part again?

I'll do a quick break down for you on the flipchart.

Some other phrases to use with flipcharts:

I'll just write that word on the flipchart for you.

We had an example of that earlier/on the previous page. Let me flip back to it.

… let me find the relevant slide.

Other expressions to use when moving between different visual aids:

Let me go back to the video and show you that clip again.

We saw that slide earlier. Just a moment while I search for it/go back to it.

… the projector doesn't seem to be working.

You may need to explain a problem you are having with visual equipment. Other expressions:

There's a problem with it.

It's not working.

I can't get it to work.

Does anyone know how it works?

Asking for help from others:

Can anyone help me with this?

Which key/switch/button do I need to press?

I'll adjust it. Is that better?

Making the slide/image clearer:

Can you move the slide down/up/sideways?

I'll focus it. Is that clearer now?

British/American differences

British	American
… can you just clarify how you worked out the numbers?	*… can you clarify how you figured out the numbers?* Note: American English does not use *just* in this sense as often as British English.
realise	*realize*
Just a moment while I search for it.	*Just a minute/second while I look for it.* (also used in British English, but sounds slightly more informal than *moment*)

Dialogues 2

Explaining a graph

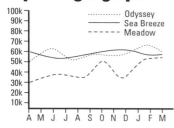

This graph shows our sales figures for the last twelve months. **The vertical axis represents sales in Australian dollars** and the figures are from April to March. **Each line on the graph shows one of our top brands**. You can see from **the key** which line represents each product. For example, the dotted line shows the sales figures for Odyssey perfume.

Using a pie chart

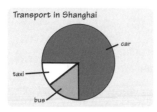

The point is illustrated in this pie chart. In Shanghai, **75 per cent of people still use a car** to get around; only 20 per cent use the bus and a much smaller 5 per cent use taxis. So, **the most popular form of public transport is still the car**.

Explaining a diagram

The new brochure has one new holiday resort in Italy. I visited it last month and I have a plan of the resort here. You can see **the apartments are at the bottom near the beach**. Each one has a balcony which looks onto the sea. The swimming pool is in the middle section. The children's play area is to the right of it and the tennis courts are in this area at the top of the plan.

Describing a flow chart

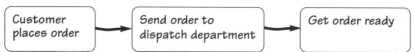

The system can be seen in this flow chart. **First, the customer places an order** with the salesperson and the **salesperson then sends the order to dispatch**. Next, the dispatch staff get the order ready and package it. Finally, a delivery service picks it up and delivers it to the customer.

Describing a table

	1.2	1.4L	1.6L	2.0Li
Audio-system		+	+	+
Sunroof		+	+	+
Security system			+	
Satellite navigation system				+

This table shows the extra features that come with the new Cheetah sports car. **The models are listed here in the top row** and the extras are listed on the left. **As you can see, our up-to-date security system does not come with the Cheetah 1.4L** but it does come with the Cheetah 1.6 L. Also, we have not included the security system as an extra feature for the Cheetah 2.0L because we are offering the satellite navigation system in its place. According to our market research, these features should give us a good position in the market place.

Notes

This graph shows our sales figures ...

Some other ways of referring to a graph:
According to the graph the number is ...
The point is illustrated in this graph.
From this graph you can see ...

The vertical axis represents sales in Australian dollars ...

This is a technical way to talk about a graph. It would be more usual and simpler to say:
vertical axis = *down the left*
The numbers down the left show the total sales in South African Rands.
horizontal axis = *along the bottom*
The months are shown along the bottom.

Each line on the graph shows one of our top brands.

Another useful phrase is:
Each line indicates the progress of a different product.

... the key ...

The *key* offers an explanation of symbols used in a graph, diagram or chart.

... 75 per cent of people still use a car ...

Sections of a pie chart can be described as percentages or fractions. For example:
25 per cent of people ...
A quarter of the people ...

... the most popular form of public transport is still the car.

These expressions compare and contrast information in a pie chart or other visual aid. Some other expressions include:
The most popular/the best selling/the fastest selling ...
The third most popular/the second biggest/the fourth largest ...
The least commonly used/the least popular ...

... the apartments are at the bottom near the beach.

A plan can be described using the examples below:
At/on the top/bottom ...
On the left/on the right ...
In the middle/centre ...
In the top/bottom left-hand corner ...
In the top/bottom right-hand corner ...

First, the customer places an order ...

Use the present tense to describe the stages of a process.

... the salesperson then sends the order to dispatch.

When describing a flow chart the order of the stages is important. Here is the language needed:
First/The first stage is ...
Then/Next/After that, ...
Finally/Lastly, ...

This table shows the extra features ...

Another way of saying this:
You can see the extra features for each model in this table.
The features of each model are clearly shown in the table.
The extra features appear in this table.

The models are listed here in the top row ...

Other phrases for describing a table:
The models are listed across the top ...
The features are listed down the side ...
On the left in the first column ...
The first and second cells ...

As you can see, our up-to-date security system does not come with the Cheetah 1.4L ...

As you will have seen ... is used here to show that the speaker expects the listeners to have already noticed key features in a graph, table or chart. Other useful expressions:
As you may have noticed ...
As you will no doubt have realised ...

British/American differences

British	American
public transport	public transportation
children's play area	children's playground (also used in British English)
send the order to dispatch	send the order to shipping/the shipping department
the dispatch staff centre	the shipping staff center

Practice

1 Put the correct preposition into the sentences below.

in	on	across	at	up	on	at	of

EXAMPLE: I'll leave this slide . up. . . . . . as I talk.

a . . . . this slide you can see the sales figures for the second quarter.

b The vertical axis represents sales . . . . Euros.

c Let's look . . . . these figures more closely.

d 33 per cent . . . . people preferred our lead brand.

e The apartments are . . . . the bottom of the plan.

f I'll just write the calculation up . . . . the flipchart.

g The models are listed . . . . the top.

2 Match the phrases on the left with the phrases on the right

1	Does anyone know	a	to be working.
2	The projector doesn't seem	b	you'll see what I mean.
3	It's interesting to note that	c	down now?
4	On the next slide	d	to the second graph.
5	Can I take this slide	e	seen that sales have peaked.
6	You will have	f	how it works?
7	Take a look at this chart and	g	the previous page.
8	There's another example on	h	you can see an outline of the main points.
9	I'd like to draw your attention	i	the number has levelled out.

3 Choose the correct verb from the box below and put it into the sentences. Make sure the verb agrees with the subject.

see	show	send	leave	place	look	be	adjust	buy

EXAMPLE: This graph . shows . . . . . the number of books sold last year.

a I'll . . . . the slide up while I talk.

b The least popular magazines . . . . the health magazines.

c Only 33 per cent of women . . . . those magazines last year.

d If you . . . . closely at this diagram, you'll see that there are seven switches.

e You can . . . . the figures on my next slide.

f Let me . . . . the projector so that you can see.

g First, the customer . . . . the order.

h Then, the salesperson . . . . the order to dispatch.

4 Put the following mini-presentations into the correct order by putting a number in the space on the left.

EXAMPLE: ..2.. Can everyone see it clearly?

..6.. Yes thanks. That's fine.

..5.. Is it better now?

..1.. OK. Here's the first slide.

..4.. I'm sorry. Let me adjust it.

..3.. No, sorry. It's not clear.

a . . . . . Finally, if the programme is correctly installed,
it will ask you to restart your computer.

. . . . . Then, they load the new software.

. . . . . First, the customer switches on their computer.

. . . . . Next, they should run the test programme to make sure that the programme is correctly installed.

b . . . . . The next is shopping.

. . . . . The third most popular is playing computer games.

. . . . . The pie chart presents the most popular activities for young people.

. . . . . As you can see, the most popular is going to nightclubs and bars.

. . . . . Therefore you can see that our product is well placed in the market.

c . . . . . In the first quarter, sales of the Aztec range rose sharply.

. . . . . In the third quarter, sales levelled out.

. . . . . Let's look at the figures more closely.

. . . . . But then sales took a dip in the second quarter.

d . . . . . You can see that the departments are listed across the top in the first row.

. . . . . If you look closely you'll see that office staff did much better this year.

. . . . . It shows the results of the company language test.

. . . . . Take a look at this table.

. . . . . and the names of those who took the test are listed on the left in the first column.

5 Put the following sentences into the correct order.

EXAMPLE: new / this / of / diagram / a / shows / plan / the / factory

This diagram shows a plan of the new factory.

1 more / look / closely / figures / let's / these / at

   . . . .

2 on / table / slide / the / can / you / next / see / the

   . . . .

3 break / for / do / I'll / down / a / you

   . . . .

4 may / sales / that / noticed / peaked / you / month / have / last

   . . . .

5 popular / is / MAXI 22 / the / model / least / the

   . . . .

6 Choose the correct word to complete each sentence.

EXAMPLE: First, the customer completes the form.   completes / completed / has completed

a The . . . . axis shows the years from 2000.   horizon / virtual / horizontal

b It's interesting to . . . . that sales peaked in January.   worry / note / surprise

c I'll help you with that. . . . .   finish / later / end

d If the slide is not clear, I'll . . . . it.   clear / change / adjust

e I have one more chart to show you before we move. . . . .   up / over / on

f Each line on the graph . . . . one of our lead brands.   represents / removes / focuses

5 Problems and Questions

Some useful phrases.
Listen to the recording and repeat.

Let me summarise the points before I go on.
What's the word I'm looking for?
Let me rephrase that.

We've almost run out of time.
Unfortunately, time won't allow me to explain all the details.
I'll just outline the last section.

Let me go back and explain.
Sorry, what I meant to say was a 20 per cent increase not a 30 per cent increase.
I'm sorry, could you rephrase your question please?
Shall I explain what I've based my numbers on?

I'll be glad to answer any questions at the end.
Actually, I'm going to talk about that later.
That's a good question and one that I'll be answering later in my talk.

I'm afraid I can't answer that question.
I'm afraid it's not my area. I suggest you speak to one of the Directors about that.
I don't think it's appropriate for me to answer that question.

Dialogues 1

Losing your place in your notes

OK. **Where was I? Let me summarise the points again before I continue**. So, there have been three main changes. First, there has been an increase in customers to our expensive stores. Second, a levelling out of visitors to our children's stores. And third a significant increase in customers to our low-price stores.

You don't know the English word

There are several problems with the new model. One problem is that it stops working if it gets … um … **what's the word I'm looking for? Let me try again**. One problem is that it stops working if it gets a little wet.

A deleted or wrong slide

If you look at the next slide, you'll see the figures are much healthier. **I'm sorry, I can't find it**. OK, **let me describe the key points to you**.

Time has run out

Unfortunately, time won't allow me to explain all the details, so I'll just outline the last section to you. The main points are on this slide. I'll explain them briefly to you.

You have forgotten to say something

The basic system will therefore cost about €50 000. **Oh, I should have said earlier that we already have** the promise of €120 000 to make this project possible. Let me go back and explain how this money became available.

Making a mistake

Ⓐ: So, if we look at last year's profit and this year's projected sales, you can see that we expect sales to double this year. Last year sales peaked in June whereas this year we expect sales to peak in September.

Ⓑ: **Sorry, but didn't sales peak in July?**

Ⓐ: Umm … . Yes, of course. **What I should have said is that** sales peaked in July.

You are unable to do something you had planned to do

OK. As you can see, the new poster for this advertising campaign is really very clever. **I wanted to give you a copy but I'm afraid the copies didn't arrive from the printers in time** for me to bring them this morning. I will post you each a copy when they arrive.

Notes

Where was I? Let me summarise the points again before I continue.

If, as sometimes happens, you lose your place, you could go back and summarise the points you have already made. This should give you time to remember what you were about to say. Another way of saying this is:
Umm … sorry, I just lost track. I'll recap the points so far.

… what's the word I'm looking for? Let me try again.

If you forget a word, don't panic. Use one of these phrases and then try to say the same thing using different words.
How do you say that in English?
Let me rephrase that.

I'm sorry, I can't find it.

If you cannot find something, use one of these expressions:
Excuse me for one moment.
I'm afraid I can't find the graph at the moment.
The slide doesn't seem to be here.

… let me describe the key points to you.

Other phrases you can use in this situation:
I'll write the main figures on the flipchart/on this slide.
Well, the key points/figures are …

Unfortunately, time won't allow me to explain all the details, …

If you are running out of time, you can also use one of these phrases to bring your presentation to an end:
Right. Now I'll conclude/end with this final point.
OK. I'll just explain this last point briefly and then there'll be time for questions.

Other phrases used to talk about time running out:
I'm sorry but time is nearly up.
We've almost run out of time.
We only have a few minutes left.

Oh, I should have said earlier that we already have …

If you forget to say something, you can always explain it by using an expression like this:
Sorry, I forgot to mention/explain …
I should have explained …

Sorry, but didn't sales peak in July?

Note how the person in the audience starts by saying *Sorry* – he doesn't want to offend the speaker.

What I should have said is that … .

Other phrases you can use if you make a mistake:
Sorry, what I meant to say was …
My mistake. What I wanted to say was …

I wanted to give you a copy, but I'm afraid the copies didn't arrive from the printers in time …

Some other similar phrases for explaining similar problems:
I planned to …, but ….
I had wanted to …, but unfortunately ….

British/American differences

British	American
a levelling out of visitors	a leveling out of visitors
Sorry, but didn't sales peak in July?	Excuse me, didn't sales peak in July? (also used in British English)
I will post you a copy	I will mail you a copy
I'm afraid I can't find the graph at the moment.	I'm afraid I can't find the graph right now.
Sorry, what I meant to say was …	Excuse me. I meant to say that … (also used in British English)

Dialogues 2

Interruptions to your talk

A: So, there are a number of changes to be introduced and I am sure they will have a positive effect on staff and customers.

B: How are you going to introduce these changes?

A: That's a good question and one that I'll be answering later in my talk.

You don't understand a question

A: Your projected figures seem to presuppose a booming economy. Is that correct?

B: I'm sorry, could you rephrase your question please?

A: The figures in your graph seem to be based on a booming – a very strong economy.

B: Yes, that's right. Shall I explain what I've based my figures on?

A: Yes please. That would be very helpful.

A question that is not on the topic

A: Could you tell me why the management got such a large pay rise this year ?

B: I'm sorry, but that's not really part of today's discussion and I'm afraid it's not a question I can answer. I suggest you speak to one of the Directors about that.

You don't know the answer to a question

A: What are your projections for the second term?

B: Erm …, I'm afraid I can't give you a full answer right now. I'll look into it and get back to you later.

An aggressive or difficult question to answer

A: Where did you get your facts from? I cannot believe that what you are saying is true!

B: Well, actually, all my facts are from company records. You're welcome to come and check the figures after the presentation if you wish.

No questions

A: So, does anyone have any questions?

Any questions at all?

No? No questions?

That's fine. If anyone wants to ask anything, please feel free to speak to me individually.

Notes

That's a good question and one that I'll be answering later in my talk.

Other expressions which can be used when someone interrupts you:

Thank you for your question. Can I answer it at the end?

That's a useful/interesting question. If you don't mind, I'd prefer to answer it at the end.

I'm sorry, could you rephrase your question please?

If you do not understand a question, you can just ask the person to repeat the question using simpler language. Here are some other phrases:

I'm sorry, could you simplify your question?
I'm sorry, I didn't understand the question. Could you repeat/rephrase it?

Shall I explain what I've based my figures on?

Shall I ... can be used to make a suggestion. Here are some more examples:

Shall I repeat my last point?
Shall I find more examples and get back to you?

... that's not really part of today's discussion ...

If someone asks you a question on a topic that is not related to your presentation, you can use one of these phrases:

I'm sorry, but I'm afraid that is not really what I have been asked to talk about today.
We're not really covering that topic today.

Really is used to sound more polite:
That's not really what we are discussing today or *That's not really what I meant.*

... I'm afraid it's not a question I can answer. I suggest you speak to one of the Directors about that.

If you are asked a question, which you cannot or should not answer, you could use one of these phrases:

That is not actually within my area. You should probably speak to the Finance Director.
That's a good question. I suggest you raise it with senior management.

... I'm afraid I can't give you a full answer right now.

Other things you can say if you don't know the answer or want to answer later:

I'm sorry. I can't answer your question right now but I'd be happy to email you an answer later.
That's an interesting point. Can I answer that after the presentation?

Well, actually, all my facts are from company records.

If someone is aggressive or they ask a difficult question, you can use one of these phrases:

I'm sorry. I'd rather not answer that question right now. Shall we talk at the end?
I'd be glad to discuss that with you later. As time is short, may I continue and we can discuss it later.
Thank you for your question. Could we discuss it at the end?

You're welcome to come and check the figures after the presentation ...

Other ways of making a polite offer:

I'd be happy to show you the figures after the presentation.
Please feel free to come and see the figures after the presentation.

So, does anyone have any questions?

Asking for questions:

Are there any questions?
Any question?
Any more questions?

British/American differences	
British	**American**
... management got such a large pay rise this year.	*... management got such a large raise this year.*
Finance Director	*CFO (Chief Financial Officer)*

Practice

1 Complete each sentence with a word on the right.

EXAMPLE: Let me .round. . . . . . up.   say / round / do

a   I'd be . . . . to email you the details later.   sorry / agree / happy

b   I'm . . . . I can't find the slide at the moment.   afraid / happy / regret

c   OK. Let me . . . . that.   reply / return / rephrase

d   Sorry, my . . . . What I meant was increase.   point / mistake / afraid

e   That's a good question. I'd actually . . . . to   probably / willing / prefer
    answer it at the end.

f   . . . . I repeat my question?   can / will / shall

g   That's not . . . . what I meant.   really / probably / definitely

2 Match a phrase on the left with the appropriate phrase on the right

1   I'm afraid it's not a topic   a   later in my talk.
2   Could you rephrase   b   to describe the details of the graph.
3   I should have said earlier   c   in English?
4   Let me go back and explain   d   for me to discuss.
5   Unfortunately time won't allow me   e   that we have already found an answer to
6   How do you say that   that question.
7   Where was I?   f   Let me summarise the main points before
8   I'll be answering that   I continue.
                                             g   how we solved the problem.
                                             h   your question please?

3 Decide whether the sentences below are correct or not. Put *C* if they are correct and *I* if they are incorrect. Try to correct them.

EXAMPLE: ..I..   I'd prefer to answer your question <u>in</u> the end.   *at*

a   . . . . .   What's the word I'm looking of ?

b   . . . . .   I'm afraid that's not my area.

c   . . . . .   I'll just explain this last point shortly.

d   . . . . .   We only have a little minutes left.

e   . . . . .   We've almost run out of time.

f   . . . . .   That was the wrong word. Let me do again.

g   . . . . .   Shall we get back to you?

h   . . . . .   Sorry, what should I have said was profit.

4 Put the following mini-dialogues into the correct order.

EXAMPLE: ..4.. and then leave a few minutes for questions.
 ..1.. Ah, we've almost run out of time.
 ..3.. I'll just explain that last point quickly.
 ..2.. I just have one main point left to present.

a ..... Right, yes and now I'll outline the action points.
 ..... So far, I've presented the survey results.
 ..1.. OK. Where was I up to?
 ..... I'll just recap the points I've already presented.
 ..... I've also explained how this applies to the five-year plan.

b ..... So, for now, I'll describe they key features to you.
 ..... The company has now bought a building for the new project.
 ..... I wanted to show you the plans but they have not arrived yet.
 ..... When they do arrive, I will send you all a copy.

c ..... But in May things improved.
 ..... OK. You can see that in March sales were down.
 ..... What's the word I'm looking for?
 ..... There was a in fact a sharp ... um ...
 ..... What's the word for *go up*?

d ..... Well, that is an overview of sales for this year.
 ..... Does anyone have any questions?
 ..... If anyone does have questions, I'm happy to talk to people individually.
 ..... So, now we have ten to fifteen minutes for questions.
 ..... Any questions at all? No?

5 Match two phrases with similar meaning.

1	I should have said earlier	a	Time has run out.
2	What's the word I'm looking for?	b	What I should have said was …
3	The time is up.	c	That's not really what I've been asked to talk about.
4	I wanted to bring the samples.	d	What's the English word for that?
5	Could you rephrase that?	e	Could you reword that?
6	That's not really part of today's discussion.	f	Let me recap the main points.
7	Let me summarise the points again.	g	I had planned to bring them.

6 Put the following sentences into the correct order.

EXAMPLE: glad / questions / I'll / any / end / very / to / be / answer / at / the

I'll be very glad to answer any questions at the end.

1 conclude / this / me / last / point / let / with

....

2 key / let / you / describe / the / to / me / points

....

3 the / you / I / speak to / about / suggest / that / finance department

....

4 that / going / I'm / later / about / actually / to / talk

....

5 planned / the / photocopier / I / handouts / wasn't / to / but / bring / working

....

6 main / write / flipchart / figures / on / I'll / the / the

....

7 more / look / closely / figures / let's / these / at

....

6 Concluding

Some useful phrases.
Listen to the recording and repeat.

In my experience, customers are interested in good service.
I think this proves that customer care is key.
I recommend the second option.

To sum up, I began by outlining the progress of the company.
Then I described the possible future trends.
In brief, there are several advantages and disadvantages to this proposal.
We need to grow and that means increasing sales.

If you need to get in touch with me, my contact details are on the screen.
Please feel free to contact me. It would be useful to have your feedback.

Well, I've covered the points I needed to present today.
Thank you for listening.
We just have time for a few questions.

As a last point, let me raise a general issue.
What we must remember is that our competitors also want to grow.
As Thomas Jefferson said: 'I find the harder I work, the more luck I seem to have.'

🔊 Dialogues 1

Making a final point

As a final point, let me raise a general issue. There has been a lot of discussion about standards of car production. If the car industry is to develop, then standards will have to be better regulated. This will cost us more money but it's something we will have to accept.

Giving your professional opinion

In my experience customers stay with a company if you give them good service. Many of our customers have given us positive feedback about our friendly and reliable service. You can see the results from our latest customer questionnaires. 63 per cent said they had returned to us more than once because of our service. **I think this proves the point that good customer service is the key to customer loyalty.**

Summarising main points

So, **to sum up, first I outlined the problem** that we face and I gave three reasons for this problem. I then presented two possible solutions. The first solution needs new equipment and therefore staff training. The second solution makes use of the equipment we already have but requires us to reduce our current staff numbers. **We now need to decide which of these two options is best for our business.**

Summarising advantages and disadvantages

OK. In brief, **there are several advantages and disadvantages. The main disadvantage is the cost to the firm** in terms of labour, equipment and capital. **On the other hand,** the advantages are increased income and increased market share.

Making a recommendation

Following what I have said today, **I recommend that we buy the second hotel. There are three reasons why I recommend this hotel. First**, it is in a good location – close to the beach. **Second**, it is already a popular hotel **and finally**, if we don't buy it, a competitor most certainly will.

Stating sources and further reading

As well as statistics from different departments in our company, **I used** examples from several useful professional journals such as *Accountancy Now*, *Business Watchdog* and *Economics for the Financial Planner*. These journals have websites providing up-to-date information. I've produced a list of addresses. If anyone wants a copy, I'll leave them here at the front.

Notes

As a final point, let me raise a general issue.
> You can also say:
> *To conclude, I'd like to introduce one final point.*
> *As a final point, I'd like to outline the projected figures for the next quarter.*

In my experience …
> Other phrases which can be used to introduce your views:
> *In my (professional) opinion …*
> *Past experience has taught me that …*

I think this proves the point that …
> Other useful phrases are:
> *Therefore, it is clear that …*
> *So, I think it's obvious that …*

… good customer service is the key to customer loyalty.
> This can also be expressed in the following ways:
> *Good customer service leads to/creates customer loyalty.*
> *Customer loyalty is the result of good customer service.*

… to sum up …
> There are a number of phrases that can introduce conclusions, some of which are as follows:
> *In brief/Finally/To conclude/*

… first I outlined the problem …
> Other useful language for summarising the main points of your presentation:
> *I gave reasons for …*
> *I then presented two possible solutions.*
> *Finally, I recommended …*

We now need to decide which of these two options is best for our business.
> You can conclude your presentation by stating what will need to be done in the near future. Other phrases:
> *So, we need to make a decision about what will benefit our company most.*
> *We need to introduce these proposals as soon as possible.*

… there are several advantages and disadvantages.
> Other phrases for introducing a similar summary:
> *There are several points on both sides.*
> *The pros and cons are as follows …*

The main disadvantage is the cost to the firm …
> Other words for *main* are *key* and *most significant*:
> *The key advantage is …*
> *The most significant disadvantage is …*

On the other hand, …
> *On the other hand* expresses contrast. It is usually used with the phrase *on the one hand* to compare two contradictory points in a discussion.
> *On the one hand we have a large number of orders. On the other hand, we do not have the staff to process them.*

… I recommend that we buy the second hotel.
> Other phrases for making your recommendation:
> *I suggest that we should buy …*
> *In my opinion we should buy …*

There are three reasons why I recommend this. First, … . Second, … and finally, … .
> This is a summary of the reasons for your recommendation and a reminder of your main points.

As well as … , I used … .
> Other similar expressions:
> *In addition to … , I also used examples/data/ideas from … .*

British/American differences

British	American
car industry	auto industry
summarising	summarizing
labour	labor

# Dialogues 2

Telling people how to contact you

A few of you may have questions after this session has finished. If you need to contact me, my email address and work number are on the screen. **Please feel free to contact me.** **It would be useful to have your feedback.**

A final summary

Finally, the demand for this programme is increasing. Our desire is to become the market leaders. We need to continue to grow and develop **and that means improving** customer care, **continuing** to focus on quality **and increasing** our customer base. We will be the market leaders. Let's pull together to achieve this goal!

Thanking people for listening

Finally, **I'd like to thank you all for taking time out of your busy day to listen to my presentation** this afternoon. I hope you will have found it useful. The important thing now is to introduce these new systems and procedures into the work place.

An informal ending

Well, **I've covered the points I needed to present today** and the time is now up. Thank you for listening. **We just have time for a few questions**. Would anyone like to raise any points?

Ending on a positive note

This company has only been in existence for four years and yet we have achieved so much. This achievement has come from all the hard work and the commitment of both management and staff. **We have a bright future, so let's work together** and see this company achieve its full potential.

Ending with a final thought

Today we have focused a lot on the company and where we want to be in the future. **What we must remember is that our competitors also want to grow** and we need to monitor their strategies and progress.

Ending with a quote

Today I have outlined our plans for the future development of the company. Our plans are ambitious and we are in no doubt that our goals can only be achieved by hard work, commitment and a little luck. **As Thomas Jefferson said,** 'I find the harder I work, the more luck I seem to have.' So, let's get out there and make a real difference.

Notes

Please feel free to contact me.

Other similar expressions include:
You're welcome to get in touch.
I'd be happy for you to speak to me.
Please email me if you have any questions.

It would be useful to have your feedback.

If you want to hear what people have to say about your talk, you can use these expressions:
I'd welcome your comments.
I'd value your thoughts on this presentation.
Please complete the feedback form.

... and that means improving ..., continuing ... and increasing ... .

When making a recommendation, you may want to give a list of key points. These points can be expressed using *that means* + the *-ing* form of the verb.
We need to improve results and that means selling more products, getting more customers and encouraging existing customers to return.

... I'd like to thank you all for taking time out of your busy day to listen to my presentation ...

Thanking people can be a good way of ending a talk. Many people like to finish by thanking the audience for coming.
Some simple examples:
Thank you for listening.
Thank you for your attention.
It was good to see you all here.
Many thanks for coming.

... I've covered the points I needed to present today ...

Other useful expressions for finishing:
That sums up my description of the new proposal.
That's the plan in theory. Now let's go and put it into practice.
It's better not to use abrupt expressions like *That's it!* or *That's all!*

We just have time for a few questions.

If time is short, you can let people know this by using words like *just, a few, one or two* or *quick.*
There's time for one or two questions.
We have time for just one more question.
Are there any quick questions or comments?

We have a bright future, so let's work together ...

Other optimistic statements to inspire your listeners!
This has been a great year. I know that you've all worked hard to achieve this. Well done!
This year is going well. We still have a lot of work to do, but we're going in the right direction.

What we must remember is that our competitors also want to grow ...

You can use *must* to give a strong suggestion. Other ways of making suggestions:
We need to remember ...
It is important that we don't forget ...

As Thomas Jefferson said, ...

Other ways of introducing a quotation:
In the words of Gandhi, ...
To quote a well-known business leader, ...
As Bill Gates once said, ...

British/American differences

British	American
programme	*program*

(As on p11 - British English uses *programme* when referring to a programme of events or a television programme but *program* for anything relating to computers.)

British	American
I hope you will have found it useful.	*I hope you have found it useful.*
focussed/focused	*focused*

Note: *focused* can be spelt either way in British English but only with a single *s* in American English.

Practice

1 **Complete each sentence by choosing the correct verb from the box. Make sure the verb is in the correct tense and agrees with the subject.**

sum	listen	remember	cover	use	have	be	improve	~~outline~~

EXAMPLE: To sum up, I .. *outlined* ...... three problems with the system.

a   We just . . . . time for a few questions.

b   I want to thank you all for . . . . today.

c   . . . . there any quick questions?

d   That . . . . up my description of the new proposal.

e   I . . . . examples from some well-known professional journals.

f   What we must . . . . is that our competitors also have a plan.

g   We need to increase sales and that means . . . . customer service.

h   Well, I've . . . . the points I needed to present today.

2 **Decide whether the sentences below are correct or not. Put *C* if they are correct and *I* if they are incorrect. Try to correct them.**

EXAMPLE: .. I ..   There are several points <u>in</u> both sides. [*on* written above *in*]

a   . . . . .   There's just time of one or two examples.

b   . . . . .   There are pros and cons on both sides.

c   . . . . .   As last point, let me raise a general question.

d   . . . . .   On the hand, there are several advantages.

e   . . . . .   In my experience, numbers usually drop at this time of year.

f   . . . . .   There are three reasons for I recommend this.

g   . . . . .   We need to increase sales and that means improving quality.

3 Complete the following sentences with the best preposition from the box.

into	for	as	with	in	~~by~~	of	up

EXAMPLE: I want to finish . . .by. . . . thanking you all.

1 So, to sum . . . . , I have presented three solutions.

2 Let's put the plan . . . . practice.

3 Please feel free to get . . . . touch . . . . me.

4 I'd be happy . . . . you to speak to me.

5 Customer loyalty is the result . . . . good customer service.

6 . . . . George Burns once said, 'Don't stay in bed, unless you can make more money in bed.'

4 Match a phrase or sentence on the left with a phrase or sentence on the right.

1 I think this proves the point that   a   of the new proposal.

2 First, I outlined the old system;   b   for a few quick questions.

3 Finally, I'd like to   c   to the organisers of this event.

4 I recommend the third option.   d   then, I explained the advantages of the new system.

5 If you need to get in touch with me,   e   lower prices mean higher sales.

6 That sums up my description   f   There are two main reasons for this.

7 A special thanks   g   my email address is on the screen.

8 There's just time   h   thank you all for listening this afternoon.

5 Complete the following concluding paragraph with appropriate words from the box.

recommend	with	~~sum~~	decide	time	listening
then	just	thank	up	next	solutions	third

So, to ① .sum.... ② ....., I explained the problem ③ . . . . the existing system and ④ . . . . presented three possible ⑤ . . . . The first solution requires new equipment, the ⑥ . . . . solution needs more staff and the ⑦ . . . . solution needs a complete change of strategy. We now need to ⑧ . . . . which solution we will select. I ⑨ . . . . the third solution because it will benefit the company for longer. Finally, I'd like to ⑩ . . . . you for ⑪ . . . . this afternoon. ⑫ . . . . is nearly up, so we ⑬ . . . . have a few minutes for questions.

6 Choose the best word to complete each sentence.

EXAMPLE: I have .. covered ...... the points I needed to.

      a covered   b spoken   c wanted   d advantage

i   This proves the point that customer service is the . . . . to customer loyalty.
    a move   b reason   c cause   d key

ii   As well as pros, there are also . . . .
    a cons   b compromise   c advantages   d negative

iii We have some time for a . . . . questions.
    a little   b few   c many   d much

iv Let's work together to see our company . . . . its potential.
    a achieve   b declare   c reward   d succeed

v   The . . . . disadvantage is the time it would take.
    a small   b large   c main   d certain

vi In the . . . . of a well-known philosopher, …
    a quotes   b words   c murmers   d said

vii Are there any . . . . questions or comments?
    a fast   b few   c quick   d less

viii That's the plan in . . . .
    a real   b idea   c sum   d theory

Glossary

1 Getting Started

Dialogues 1

It's good to have Miguel Ferreira here. . . . .

Thank you Paul. It's great to be back. . . . .

Hello. Thank you all for coming. . . . .

Please help yourselves. . . . .

Right. If everyone's ready, let's start. . . . .

As you all know, I'm the Head of the . . . .

   Design Department. . . . .

I'm talking to you today as the manager . . . .

   of the team. . . . .

By the end of this session you'll know . . . .

   about the new product. . . . .

How do we avoid problems? . . . .

I read something interesting the other day. . . . .

Dialogues 2

Sam asked me to present my ideas. . . . .

Today I'd like to present a solution. . . . .

I hope that you'll give your ideas and comments. . . . .

If there is anything else you'd like to bring up, ...

   we can talk about it at the end. . . . .

First, I'd like to outline the main areas of growth. . . . .

If you have any questions, please feel free . . . .

   to stop me. . . . .

I'll leave fifteen or twenty minutes at the . . . .

   end for questions. . . . .

Please take one. . . . .

I have a handout with the main points of . . . .

   my presentation. . . . .

2 Moving on

Dialogues 1

	Your language
We must ask ourselves these questions.	. . . .
I'll answer each of these questions one by one.	. . . .
The first problem is call-response times.	. . . .
That's an overall look at the marketing campaign.	. . . .
Now, let's take a more detailed look.	. . . .
There are three options.	. . . .
We can continue as we are.	. . . .
In my opinion, we are in a strong financial position.	. . . .
If we build now, we will be ready for the expansion.	. . . .
I said earlier that security wasn't very good last year.	. . . .
I'd now like to change direction.	. . . .

Dialogues 2

Unfortunately, the number of new customers was below target.	. . . .
The good news is that we've nearly doubled sales.	. . . .
OTC stands for over-the-counter drugs.	. . . .
That's the time it takes someone to answer the phone in our call centre.	. . . .
In short, we need to improve our customer service.	. . . .
We will produce the new software.	. . . .
We may find ourselves marketing it in a different way.	. . . .
To sum up, last month's sales doubled.	. . . .
This is excellent for this time of year.	. . . .
Next I'd like to move on and look at the sales.	. . . .

3 Numbers

Dialogues 1 | Your language

Sixty-nine per cent of male shoppers. . . . .

Two-thirds of the people said that they
liked the new colours. . . . .

We hope to have 1 530 in nine schools. . . . .

The temperature must be between 4.3°
and 5.6° centigrade. . . . .

We'll make a loss of €50 000 this year. . . . .

Next year we expect to break even. . . . .

We expect to make a profit. . . . .

You can see this number in the third
column: - 50 000. . . . .

Around 300 people answered our questionnaire. . . . .

About 30 per cent were between eighteen
and forty. . . . .

Dialogues 2

The chart shows a significant rise in the
number of companies. . . . .

This year the number has gone up to seventy. . . . .

There has been a decrease in the number
of people with more than one child. . . . .

The number of children going to primary
school will also fall. . . . .

The number of staff has stayed the same. . . . .

Sales of Brighter Smile toothpaste peaked
in May. . . . .

Sales are still below prediction. . . . .

There'll be a dramatic rise in private
car owners. . . . .

Sales dropped dramatically. . . . .

Sales began to increase gradually. . . . .

Sales stayed more or less the same. . . . .

4 Visual Aids

Dialogues 1

Your language

You can see from this slide that I'm going to cover three points. . . . .

. . . .

I'll leave this up as I talk. . . . .

On the next slide you can see the new model. . . . .

Let's look at these figures more closely. . . . .

It's interesting to note that the increase in sales happened after our campaign. . . . .

. . . .

I'll do a quick break down for you on the flipchart. . . . .

. . . .

Let me find the relevant slide. . . . .

The projector doesn't seem to be working. . . . .

Does anyone know how it works? . . . .

I'll adjust it. Is that better? . . . .

Dialogues 2

This graph shows our sales figures. . . . .

The vertical axis represents sales in Australian dollars. . . . .

. . . .

Each line on the graph features one of our top brands. . . . .

. . . .

75 per cent of people still use a car. . . . .

. . . .

The most popular form of public transport is still the car. . . . .

. . . .

The apartments are at the bottom near the beach. . . . .

. . . .

First, the customer places an order. . . . .

The salesperson then sends the order to dispatch. . . . .

. . . .

This table shows the extra features. . . . .

The models are listed here in the top row. . . . .

As you can see, our up-to-date security system does not come with the Cheetah 1.4L. . . . .

. . . .

5 Problems and questions

Dialogues 1

Where was I? Let me summarise the points
again before I continue.

What's the word I'm looking for?

Let me try again.

I'm sorry, I can't find it.

Let me describe the key points to you.

I'm sorry but time is nearly up.

Unfortunately, time won't allow me to explain
all the details.

Oh, I should have said earlier that we already
have €120 000.

Let me go back and explain how the money
became available.

What I should have said is that we have
doubled sales this year.

I wanted to give you a copy but the copies
did not arrive from the printers in time.

Dialogues 2

That's a good question and one that I'll be
answering later in my talk.

I'm sorry, could you rephrase your question
please?

Shall I explain what I've based my figures on?

That's not really part of today's discussion.

I'm afraid it's not a topic for me to discuss.

I suggest you speak to someone in the Human
Resources department about that.

I'm afraid I can't give you a full answer now.

Well, actually, all my facts are from company
records.

You're welcome to come and check the figures
after the presentation.

Your language

....
....
....
....
....
....
....
....
....
....
....
....
....
....
....

....
....
....
....
....
....
....
....
....
....
....

6 Concluding

Dialogues 1

	Your language
As a last point, let me raise a very general problem.	. . . .
In my experience, customers stay with the company if we give good service.	. . . .
Good customer service is the key to customer loyalty.	. . . .
First I outlined the problem, I then presented two possible solutions.	. . . .
We now need to decide which of these two options is best for our business.	. . . .
There are several advantages and disadvantages.	. . . .
The main disadvantage is the cost to the firm.	. . . .
On the other hand, the advantages are increased income and increased market share.	. . . .
I recommend that we buy the second hotel.	. . . .
There are three reasons why I recommend this. First, … . Second, … and finally, … .	. . . .
As well as statistics, I used examples from several useful professional journals.	. . . .

Dialogues 2

Please feel free to get in touch.	. . . .
It would be useful to hear your feedback.	. . . .
That means improving …, continuing … and increasing … .	. . . .
I'd like to thank you all for taking time out of your busy day to listen to my presentation.	. . . .
I've covered the points I needed to present today.	. . . .
We just have time for a few questions.	. . . .
What we must remember is that our competitors also want to grow.	. . . .
As Thomas Jefferson said … .	. . . .

Answers

1 Getting started

1 1 c 2 d 3 g 4 e 5 b 6 a 7 h 8 f

2 a have b present c take d like e leave f introduce

3 a on b by c from d at e on f By g as

4 1 I have a handout with the main points of my presentation.
2 I'm here to explain customer care.
3 Good morning. I'm Mohammed from the Malaysian office.
4 I read something interesting the other day.
5 To begin with, I'd like to outline the proposal.
6 As I'm sure you know, I'm the project leader.

5 a get b worry c help d free e describe f focus

6 *Possible answers*
1 Thank you. I'm glad to be here.
2 If we're all here, let's begin. / If everyone's here, I'll begin.
3 Please take a handout.
4 First, I'll explain the problems with the old process. After that, I'll explain the new process.
5 I plan to leave time for questions at the end.

7 1 here/ready 2 let's 3 from 4 know 5 glad/happy/pleased 6 like 7 present/outline
8 First 9 Then/Next/After that 10 finally 11 time 12 have 13 take

2 Moving on

1 1 c 2 d 3 b 4 d 5 b 6 c 7 a

2 1 g 2 e 3 a 4 h 5 c 6 b 7 d 8 f

3 i In other words ii First iii Next; Second iv Third; Finally v For example vi As a result

4 a What b How c Does d Why e How f Where g Why

5 1 were 2 explained 3 had 4 sold 5 mentioned

6 1 What do you know about our new product?
2 How can we increase sales?
3 Who is going to buy our product?
4 What is the new product?
5 When can we complete the changes?
6 Where shall we start?

7 1 I think 2 In short 3 As a result of this 4 Again 5 For instance

3 Numbers

1 1 (a / one) quarter of all shoppers
2 forty-five dollars (and) seventy cents
3 seven-eighths of all men
4 thirty-five per cent of children
5 minus sixty-five point oh two
6 four hundred and twenty-three thousand
7 two thirds of the population
8 two hundred and forty-three

2 a More than   b than   c over   d Just under/less than   e Roughly/around
f Less than/just under

3 1 Sales stayed the same.
2 Sales dropped dramatically.
3 Sales declined steadily.
4 Sales peaked.

4 *Possible answers*
a Sales of Stay Fresh washing powder fell sharply.
b Ticket sales rose significantly.
c The number of dog owners decreased gradually.
d (The number of) complaints doubled.
e Petrol consumption dropped steadily.
f The number of private cars increased dramatically.
g (The number of) sales levelled out.

5 a i to   ii rose/increased   iii to rise/increase   iv in   v out   vi was   vii peaked
b i prediction   ii made   iii break   iv expect   v profit
c i predict   ii next   iii in   iv less   v as   vi following

4 Visual Aids

1 a on   b in   c at   d of   e at   f on   g across

2 1 f   2 a   3 i   4 h   5 c   6 e   7 b   8 g   9 d

3 a leave   b are   c bought   d look   e see   f adjust   g places   h sends

4 a   4   Finally, if the programme is correctly installed, it will ask you to restart your computer.
2   Then, they load the new software.
1   First, the customer switches on their computer.
3   Next, they should run the test programme to make sure that the programme is correctly installed.

b   3   The next is shopping.
    4   The third most popular is playing computer games.
    1   The pie chart presents the most popular activities for young people.
    2   As you can see, the most popular is going to nightclubs and bars.
    5   Therefore you can see that our product is well placed in the market.

c   2   In the first quarter, sales of the Aztec range rose sharply.
    4   In the third quarter, sales levelled out.
    1   Let's look at the figures more closely.
    3   But then sales took a dip in the second quarter.

d   3   You can see that the departments are listed across the top in the first row
    5   If you look closely you'll see that the staff did much better this year.
    2   It shows the results of the company language test.
    1   Take a look at this table.
    4   and the names of those who took the test are listed on the left in the first column.

5   1   Let's look more closely at these figures.
        2   You can see the table on the next slide.
        3   I'll do a break down for you.
        4   You may have noticed that sales peaked last month.
        5   The MAXI 22 is the least popular model.

6   a horizontal b note c later d adjust e on f represents

5 Problems and questions

1   a happy b afraid c rephrase d mistake e prefer f shall g really

2   1 d   2 h   3 e   4 g   5 b   6 c   7 f   8 a

3   a I   *of* should be *for*
        b C
        c I   *shortly* should be *briefly*
        d I   *little* should be *few*
        e C
        f I   *do* should be *try*
        g C
        h I   *should I* should be *I should*

4   a   5   Right, yes and now I'll outline the action points.
            3   So far, I've presented the survey results.
            1   OK. Where was I up to?
            2   I'll just recap the points I've already presented.
            4   I've also explained how this applies to the five-year plan.

b 3 So, for now, I'll describe they key features to you.
  1 The company has now bought a building for the new project.
  2 I wanted to show you the plans but they have not arrived yet.
  4 When they do arrive, I will send you all a copy.

c 2 But in May things improved.
  1 OK. You can see that in March sales were down.
  4 What's the word I'm looking for?
  3 There was a in fact a sharp … um …
  5 What's the word for *go up*?

d 1 Well, that is an overview of sales for this year.
  3 Does anyone have any questions?
  5 If anyone does have questions, I'm happy to talk to people individually.
  2 So, now we have ten to fifteen minutes for questions.
  4 Any questions at all? No?

5 1 b 2 d 3 a 4 g 5 e 6 c 7 f

6 1 Let me conclude with this last point.
  2 Let me describe the key points to you.
  3 I suggest you speak to the finance department about that.
  4 I'm actually going to talk about that later.
  5 I planned to bring handouts but the photocopier wasn't working.
  6 I'll write the main figures on the flipchart.
  7 Let's look more closely at these figures.

6 Concluding

1 a have b listening c Are d sums e used f remember g improving h covered

2 a I   *of* should be *for*
  b C
  c I   As *a* last point
  d I   On the o*ther* hand
  e C
  f I   *for* should be *why*
  g C

3 1 up 2 into 3 in; with 4 for 5 of 6 As

4 1 e 2 d 3 h 4 f 5 g 6 a 7 c 8 b

5 1 sum 2 up 3 with 4 then 5 solutions 6 next 7 third 8 decide 9 recommend
  10 thank 11 listening 12 Time 13 just

6 i d ii a iii b iv a v c vi b vii c viii d